Meet the Pirates

Christy Judah

Meet the Pirates

By Christy Judah

ISBN-13: 978-1466342767
ISBN-10: 1466342765

Published by Coastal Books
C. 2011 by Joyce C. Judah

<u>Additional Books by this Author</u>
An Ancient History of Dogs: Spaniels through the Ages
Building a Basic Foundation for Search and Rescue Dog Training
Buzzards and Butterflies: Human Remains Detection Dogs
Water Search: Search and Rescue Dogs Finding Drowned Persons
Building a Search and Rescue Team from the Ground Up
Search and Rescue Canine Training Log & Journal
Search and Rescue Training Log & Journal
Brunswick County: The Best of the Beaches
The Faircloth Family History:
A Compilation of Resources and Genealogy
The Legends of Brunswick County
More Legends
Two Faces of Dixie: Politicians, Plantations and Slaves
Meet the Search and Rescue Dogs
Meet the Police Dogs

Contact Information: (910) 842-7942
www.christyjudah.com
christyjudah@atmc.net

Printed in the United States of America.

Meet the Pirates

"A pirate ship's cannon fires a warning blast. The explosion rocks a nearby merchant ship. Musket balls fly. Grenades explode. A wounded helmsman staggers. He lets go of the ship's wheel, and the ship swings around crazily. Flames flicker everywhere. Pistols fire."

"Pirates, screaming threats, board the merchant ship, swinging axes and cutlasses (short, curved swords). Hissing through his teeth, Blackbeard—one of the most dreaded pirates who ever lived—jumps to the deck. He stands tall and lean. Pieces of rope burn like fuses among coils of his black hair. Sashes stuffed with pistols and daggers crisscross his huge chest. Black ribbons flap from the braids in his beard. Terrified sailors flee. Blackbeard and his fierce crew have pirated another ship."[i]

Blackbeard and many other men and women attacked other ships and robbed them of their jewelry, money and valuables. They were feared by all and thought to be the meanest and most evil people living in their time. Stealing is wrong and these scoundrels were wanted by the officials for their wrongdoing.

The pirates sailed the seas on large ships looking for other ships which might be carrying valuables to steal. The tall masts on the boats flew specially designed pirate flags. These flags were called the "Jolly Roger," and every pirate had one.

This is the flag of a pirate named *Edward England*. Edward was born in England but his real last name was Seegar. Ironically, Edward died as a very poor man at a young age. [iii]

Pirates would steal valuables and then sell them to others. The Pirate *Avary* is shown selling his jewels in the following engraving dated about 1887.

Pirates are known to have traveled the Carolina coast and many reports of their escapes remain to attest to their activities. Among those was...

The Meanest Pirate
Captain William Kidd
(1654-1701)

v

Captain William Kidd was born about 1654-65 and was said to have buried a chest of treasure in the area of Winnabow, North Carolina in Brunswick County. Other chests of treasure were said to have been buried in Long Island, New York; areas that welcomed pirates about 1699.

His name, Captain Kidd, has come down through the years as a symbol of piracy. Ironically, Captain Kidd had originally been employed to rid the seas of pirates.

Kidd was eventually captured. From his farewell speech he left these words:

"My name was Captain Kidd, when I sail'd, when I sail'd,
and so wickedly I did (ignore the) laws I did forbid,
When I sail'd, when I sail'd.
I roam'd from sound to sound, and many a ship I found,
And then I sunk or burn'd, When I sail'd."

"I murder'd William Moore, and laid him in his gore,
Not many leagues from shore, When I sail'd.
Farewell to young and old, all jolly seamen bold.
You're welcome to my gold, for I must die, I must die."

"Farewell to Lunnon town. The pretty girls all round,
No pardon can be found, and I must die, I must die,
Farewell, for I must die."

"Then to eternity, in hideous misery,
I must lie, I must lie."

Captain William Kidd welcoming a young woman on board his ship; other men and women crowd the deck as another woman steps aboard.[vi]

Thirty years later the profession was beginning to wane but before that time the likes of Samuel Bellamy and others sailed the southern coast of North Carolina.[viii] [ix]

The Romantic Pirate Samuel Bellamy (1689-1717)

Captain Samuel Bellamy had a last name that was and still is quite common in Brunswick County. He sailed up and down the North and South Carolina coastline regularly. He was later called "Black Bellamy" and was known as one of the most active freebooters.

(A freebooters: n. A person who pillages and plunders, especially a pirate.)[x]

On his seaboard journey, he stopped in Eastham Harbor, Massachusetts, where he met a local beauty, 15-year-old girl named Maria Hallett. Her parents liked Samuel, but they did not think that the poor self-confident sailor was good enough for their daughter. With his friend, Paulsgrave Williams, he set sail with a promise that he'd return as the respected Captain of the greatest ship that world has ever seen! So she waited for him. xi

*Many months passed, but Samuel and Williams could not find Spanish treasure. Disappointed, but still willing to risk everything to get rich, Samuel and Williams decided to join Captain Benjamin Hornigold's pirate crew.*xii

Hornigold was a capable Captain, who was famous for his generosity to prisoners. But in June of 1716, the crew revolted against him and Samuel Bellamy was elected the new Captain. Bellamy proved to be a very successful pirate. In one year, he and his men robbed more than fifty ships, mainly in the Atlantic and the Caribbean.

Captain Samuel Bellamy, known as *Black Bellamy*, was a tall, strong, well-mannered and a very tidy man. He liked expensive clothes, especially black coats. The crew liked him a lot and sometimes even called him "Pirate Robin Hood".

Eventually he captured and took control of a ship called the *Whydah*. When he and his crew took control of the *Whydah*, it contained a lot of gold and silver; more than they could ever have hoped to steal in 20 years of work. Bellamy kept the *Whydah* for himself and gave his other ships to his crew. Since everyone on the crew now had plenty of gold and silver, many of his men decided to retire and live the rest of their lives as normal folks in quaint little towns up and down the eastern coast. With riches untold, they headed to their new homes.

However, the *Whydah* was caught in an intense storm in the late afternoon of April 26th near Cape Cod as it traveled back to reunite with Bellamy's girl, Maria Hallet. There was a thick fog, rain and strong winds…perhaps it was a hurricane? [xv]

By the morning there were only pieces of the *Whydah* floating in the bay. The ship ran into a sandbar off the coast of Cape Cod,

Massachusetts as large waves crashed over the ship snapping the main mast. The ship broke in half and sank. The pilot swam to shore and was one of the few men who survived.

The treasure on board sank to the bottom of the sea. Eight of the pirates survived the crash and two told the stories of the Prince of Pirates on the *Whydah*. One of those was Thomas Davis, a Welsh carpenter.

Davis passed down the accounts of the Cape Cod shipwreck and the piracy legend of the *Whydah* and it's crew.

Bellamy was fond of fine clothes like Stede Bonnet and wore four pistols in the sash over his velvet coat. He tied his long dark hair with a black bow."[xvi] But died just the same after being convicted of his crimes.

The Gentleman Pirate
Stede Bonnet
(1688-1718)

Nearby Southport became the home, albeit temporary, of one of the county's most famous pirates, Stede Bonnet. He came from an old and respected family and was previously a planter in Barbados. Bonnet sailed the *Royal James* through Virginia and Delaware and southward to the Cape Fear River. Stede Bonnet was not the typical pirate but a man who had a successful career in the military and a large plantation. However, he turned pirate…perhaps because of his wife's nagging some have surmised.

With no experience in sailing, he never quite learned how to become a mean and evil pirate until he met *Blackbeard*, a more experienced and dangerous man. At one point Bonnet convinced Blackbeard to allow him to command the ship the *Revenge*. Soon after, the two parted. Bonnet left for the town of Bath where he surrendered to the Governor of North Carolina, Charles Eden, as a reformed pirate.

This act however did not quell Bonnets desire for piracy, and he continued to scour the sea for vessels and treasure.

Flag of Stede Bonnet

Stede Bonnet, sometimes called the *Gentleman Pirate*, was repairing his vessel in a nearby creek when he was captured. Bonnet's Creek was a haven for Stede Bonnet who operated in the area and was captured in the harbor during the Battle of the Sand Bar in 1718, a furious battle with Col. William Rhett. Rhett was sent to find and capture Bonnet and his ships. Bonnet finally surrendered to Rhett but prior to his capture, he buried three chests of treasure on the shoreline of an inlet close to the mouth of the Cape Fear River. The reported location is near the end of the peninsula.

Folklore says the Cape Fear was a popular rendezvous for pirates and they came in large numbers, although Stede Bonnet was the only one known to use the Cape Fear River regularly, in what is now Brunswick County.

It is said that some of Bonnet's men escaped this final roundup in the Cape Fear and formed the first settlement of the Cape Fear area about 1725, joined by a group of Lumbee Indians. Stede was brought to trial for his crimes in Charles Town (Charleston), South Carolina. Where he was found guilty of all charges.

The Brunswick County Pirate
Captain William Hewett
(C. 1660 -1718)

Captain Hewett was a member of Stede Bonnet's crew and sailed the Cape Fear/New Hanover/Brunswick seas. As a member of Bonnet's crew, he later joined Blackbeard to terrorize sea going vessels. He was eventually convicted of his crimes in Charleston, South Carolina, in 1718, along with his fellow crewmembers and Stede himself.

It is interesting to note that he may have owned a plantation on the Charleston's Cooper River in South Carolina as some matching surnames appear in that area on local census records. The same surname also appears on the 1670 Census of Jamaica where a John Hewitt owned 800 acres. Were some of the descendents of the Hewett/Hewitt pirate family relocated to the Jamaica area with treasures untold and eventual heirs of many hundreds of acres of land? Legend does not provide us with the whole story. Only speculation remains, but in his trial, being accused of stealing from other ships, William Hewett said,

"I design'd to go to St. Thomas with Major Bonnet for he told me he was bound thither; I was willing to go with him."

All the pirates tried for their crimes that December day in 1718 were found guilty because each had a share of the booty and treasures, which had been stolen from other ships. Hewett was buried at the low-water mark at White Point near Charleston, South Carolina.

**The Most Famous Pirate
Edward Teach
"Blackbeard"
(1680- 1718)**

xviii

Edward Teach, known as *Blackbeard*, was perhaps the most famous pirate of all-time. His was most at home in the Ocracoke Island area in northeastern North Carolina near the Virginia border. However, locals around the Holden Beach area still whisper stories passed down for generations. Several times in the past hundred years, his ghost was "almost" spotted near the Lockwood Folly River. Throughout the Carolina coast, the keen eye can still see *Blackbeard* in the dark of the moon especially in the fall as the temperatures cool from the summer's heat.

Blackbeard terrorized the coastline from 1716-1718. He and his crew would ambush ships carrying passengers and steal their cargo like other pirates of their time.

Blackbeard sailed in and out of the Cape Fear inlet often hiding around Topsail Island. *Teach* was captured and returned to Bath in 1718.

"In 1718 Alexander Spotswood, the Governor of Virginia, was under enormous pressure to remove pirates from his domain, so he offered rewards for their capture. At the top of the wanted list was Blackbeard with £100 on his head. Spotswood was worried that pirates were increasingly harboring in the Pamlico Sound naturally protected by the barrier islands of the Outer Banks, and accessed by the Ocracoke Inlet. There was even talk of buccaneers fortifying Ocracoke Island itself to make a more imposing base." [xix]

Blackbeard's Flag

"Spotswood enlisted the help of two experienced buccaneer hunters: - Captains Maynard and Hyde. They were both keen to pursue Blackbeard but their ships were unsuitable for the shallow inlets around the Pamlico Sound. Robert Maynard captained the first sloop, the *Jane*, and took command of the expedition of 60 men; Captain Hyde assisted in the *Ranger*."

Blackbeard meets Robert Maynard.

"Once Blackbeard's whereabouts was known, the party set sail and arrived at the Ocracoke Inlet on the evening of the 21st of October, 1718. A local pilot guided the sloops through the sandbars and shoals protecting the anchorage, and the *Adventure* was sighted late in the evening. It was decided that a morning attack would take advantage of the after effects of the night's revelry on board the pirate vessel."

"Blackbeard, unaware of the impending fight, only had a crew of 19 on board and spent the evening ... with some of his men." "In the morning Maynard and Hyde cautiously moved into the Sound following a small boat taking depth soundings. An observant lookout quickly raised the alarm, and a volley of shot peppered the expedition's boats as the *Adventure* slipped anchor. Maynard and Hyde were soon in hot pursuit but in the rush both their sloops ran aground. The three vessels were close enough for a shouted exchange to take place, and Blackbeard mocked Maynard and his men making it clear that he would be taking no prisoners." "As the tide rose the two sloops were freed; the wind was so slack that they had to resort to oars. The *Adventure* fired ... close range broadside of shot mixed with nails decimating the party and the *Ranger* was put out of the fight..."

"Maynard attacked; a volley of shot crippled the *Adventure* by bringing down sails and masts. Maynard had craftily hidden most of his men below decks, so as the two boats ran together Blackbeard boarded with 10 of his pirates thinking his earlier fire wiped out the crews."

A ... struggle ensued as the hidden crew streamed up through the hatches attacking Blackbeard's men and knocking them down in their wake. Maynard and Blackbeard were soon involved in a desperate struggle.

"The crew of the *Adventure* continued to fight for their lives but the *Ranger* finally rallied and got back into the battle. Despite the desperate fight of the pirates the battle was soon over and a number of prisoners taken, the *Adventure* was secured…"   The battle was over.

"The end of Blackbeard and the trial of the remaining crew was the beginning of the end of the years of buccaneering glory, and a big coup in the war against piracy." [xxxxi]

Throughout the 21st century, modern explorers have continued to search for sunken pirate ships, particularly Blackbeard's, *Queen Anne Revenge*. In October of 2007, archaeologists recovered a 2,500 pound cannon from the ship. The *Queen Anne's Revenge* was believed to have sunk in the Beaufort Inlet about 1719 when it ran aground. The treasure below attests to the presence of pirates off the shores of the Carolina's and continued efforts at recovery of items from this flagship of Blackbeard have produced Pewter platters, ornamental brass items, shards of ceramics and glass, a small rail cannon, and considerable amounts of lead shot and gold dust. Archaeologists expect to recover over 1,000 items, and perhaps eventually, over tens of thousands of individual artifacts.

Cannon, bronze bell and jug recovered from the Queen Anne's Revenge, Blackbeard's ship.

Queen Anne Revenge

The Married Pirates
Jacob & Ann Johnson

Another set of Brunswick County pirates known to have been in the area about ten years later was Jacob Johnson and his wife, Ann, circa 1724. They were caught and charged with having "feloniously stolen goods and wares and merchandise belonging to Peter Pedro of Cape Fear, who recently died."[xxv]

Interestingly, there were no land grants to a Peter Pedro at that time. But there was a stream on the west side of the river known as Perdreau's Creek which most likely was named after Peter Pedro or one of his relatives. It later became Orton Creek.

The Fort Caswell Pirate
Mary Anne Blythe

"One of the most romantic female pirates was Mary Ann Blythe, who was Blackbeard's second-in-command! She was originally one of his captives, but refused to cower in fear and actually struck him across the face. He liked her spirit, and taught her everything he knew. She's famous for becoming as good a pirate as he was, but ultimately she fell in love with a Spaniard she had captured. The two slipped away in a yacht that she had captured, and were never seen again."[xxvi]

Mary Anne Blythe, the female buccaneer, supposedly buried her treasure in the area of old Fort Caswell, at the mouth of the Cape Fear River. It has yet to be discovered. Another cache is reportedly on Plum Point in Beaufort County, a chest full of jewels.

A cache of pirate treasure was removed from the ground at Plum Point in 1928 and it was attributed to her. Is there more? She is but one of the known women pirates as tough and vicious as their male counterparts.

Pirates burying their treasure.

**The Lady Pirate
Anne Bonny**
(1700-1782)

Anne Bonny, born in Ireland, dressed as a boy, pretending to be a son to her father's friends. Her father was a successful lawyer and merchant and bought a plantation in the new land. Upon her mother's death, Anne took over the duties as her father's housekeeper and grew into a hardy girl with a fierce and courageous temper.

She eventually married James Bonny whom her father described as "not worth a groat." Later she left him to be with Jack Rackham and the two took to the sea, Anne disguised in men's clothing.

The Calico Pirate
Jack Rackham
(1680-1720)

John Rackham, often called "Calico Jack," acquired his ship, the *Treasure*, through neglect by the former commander. Mary Read and Anne Bonny, the best-known female pirates, sailed with him on this ship. The two "ladies" eventually took control of his ship.

"John Rackham, who earned the nickname "Calico Jack" because of his taste for clothes made of brightly-colored Indian Calico cloth, was an up-and-coming pirate during the years when piracy was rampant in the Caribbean and Nassau was the capital of a pirate kingdom of sorts."[xxviii]

His ship was captured in November of 1720 and nearly its entire crew, including Rackham, was convicted of their thieving crimes.

Mary Read
(1690 -1721)

Mary Read was a fierce pirate and would attempt any hazardous task. She cursed and swore with the best of the men. She dressed as the male pirates, in men's jackets, trousers and a handkerchief tied around her head.

"While en route to the West Indies, Read's ship was attacked and captured by pirates. Read decided to join them and for a while lived the life of a pirate in the Caribbean before accepting the king's pardon in 1718. Like many former pirates, she signed on board a privateer commissioned to hunt down those buccaneers who had not accepted the pardon. It didn't last long, as the whole crew soon took over the ship. By 1720 she had found her way on board the pirate ship of "Calico Jack" Rackham."[xxix]

She was captured by Captain Burnet, tried and imprisoned but later released. Shortly thereafter she disappeared, never to be seen again. The same thing happened to Anne Bonny and she was also released to disappear into the world.

Mary Read eventually died of a fever in prison, not long after her trial...about 1721.

xxx

Modern Pirates

Although some claim that modern descendents of the aforementioned pirates are still among the eastern coasts of North Carolina, make no mistake that every young boy wants to dress as a pirate at least once in his life.

Arrrggghhh, Matey!

Captain Isaih D. Fisher[xxxi]

End Notes

[i] http://www.nationalgeographic.com/pirates/bbeard.html
[ii] *Fight between the French Confiance (Robert Surcouf) and the HMS Kent. Drawing by Ambroise-Louis Garnera (1783-1857)*
[iii] *Flag of Edward England.*
[iv] *Engraving by Aikmann. Avary sells his Jewels. Originally published in Pyle, Howard (June-November 1887). Sourced from Johnson, Merle De Vore (1921) in the Buccaneers and Marooners of the Spanish Main. New York, United States, and London, United Kingdom: Harper and Brothers. (Pyle – 1853-1911).*
[v] *Pyle, Howard illustration of Captain Kidd burying treasure.*
[vi] *Ferris, Jean Leon Gerome (1863-1930) oil on canvas. Captain Kidd in New York Harbor. Reproduction number LC_USZC2-6373. Postcard published by the Foundation Press, Inc., in 1932. Reproduction of oil painting from series: The Pageant of a Nation.*
[vii] *Kidd on the Deck okf the Adventure Galley: illustration dated before 1911 by Pyle, Howard, Johnson, Merle De Vore (1921) in Howard Pyle's Book of Pirates: Fiction, Fact & Fancy Concerning the Buccaneers & Marooners of the Spanish Main, P. 84, New York, United States, and London. Harper and Brothers.*
[viii] http://www.amazon.com/gp/product/B001BZZX5U?ie=UTF8&tag=thepiratesrea-20&link_code=as3&camp=211189&creative=373489&creativeASIN=B001BZZX5U
[ix] http://www.google.com/imgres?q=samuel+bellamy+pirate&hl=en&sa=X&rlz=1T4ADRA_enUS414US414&tbm=isch&prmd=imvnso&tbnid=oAJLXMMu6sHDsM:&imgrefurl=http://www.wix.com/samuelbellamy/ylksbwebsiteoct2010/prince&docid=cemXdInwCXBnHM&w=256&h=253&ei=_9tvTp-ECYWztwe3qdDiCQ&zoom=1&iact=hc&vpx=781&vpy=150&dur=1573&hovh=202&hovw=204&tx=99&ty=218&page=2&tbnh=142&tbnw=144&start=44&ndsp=39&ved=1t:429,r:23,s:44&biw=1920&bih=837
[x] *Wilczynski, Krzysztof.*
[xi] http://www.thewayofthepirates.com/famous-pirates/samuel-bellamy.php
[xii] http://www.thewayofthepirates.com/famous-pirates/samuel-bellamy.php
[xiii] http://www.geocaching.com/seek/cache_details.aspx?guid=b7a672f0-3870-4f0c-a525-7f173e68497b
[xiv] http://www.geocaching.com/seek/cache_details.aspx?guid=34a89893-936e-4860-9ef8-3536830524a5
[xv] http://www.1st-art-gallery.com/Andreas-Achenbach/Ships-In-A-Storm-On-The-Dutch-Coast-1854.html
[xvi] http://www.thepiratesrealm.com/Samuel%20Bellamy.html
[xvii] http://www.thewayofthepirates.com/gallery/famous_pirates/stede_bonnet/stede_bonnet.jpg
[xviii] *Illustration by Don Maitz.*
[xix] *Hill, Jerry.*
[xx] *Hill, Jerry. Blackbeard's Last Stand, Cordingly, David "Life among the Pirates" 1995. Exquemelin. A.O."The Buccaneers of America", 1923. Ocracoke Island Web Site www.ocracokeisland.com.*

[xxi] http://www.friendsofqar.org/
[xxii] *Cannon from the Queen Anne's Revenge.* http://www.qaronline.org/artifacts/cannonC21.htm
[xxiii] *English: An Accurate Map of North and South Carolina With Their Indian Frontiers, Shewing in a distinct manner all the Mountains, Rivers, Swamps, Marshes, Bays, Creeks, Harbours, Sandbanks and Soundings on the Coasts; with The Roads and Indian Paths; as well as The Boundary or Provincial Lines, The Several Townships and other divisions of the Land in Both the Provinces; the whole from Actual Surveys By Henry Mouzon and Others. 1775.*
[xxiv] *Jean Leon Gerome Ferris (1863–1930. 1920 Illustration depicting the battle between Blackbeard the Pirate and Lt. Maynard in Ocracoke Bay, NC about 1718.*

[xxv] Lee, Lawrence. The History of Brunswick County, NC.
[xxvi] http://answers.yahoo.com/question/index?qid=20101211114700AAFLuv8
[xxvii] Sketch of Anne Bonney. http://www.elizabethanenglandlife.com/anne-bonny-famous-woman-pirate.html
[xxviii] http://latinamericanhistory.about.com/od/historyofthecaribbean/p/Biography-Of-John-Calico-Jack-Rackham.htm
[xxix] http://latinamericanhistory.about.com/od/Pirates/p/Biography-Of-Mary-Read.htm
[xxx] Mary Read.
[xxxi] ,Isaih D. Fisher, son of Jonathan and Jennifer Fisher. Grandson of the Author. October 2007.

**This book is dedicated to my grandsons, Isaih, Jacob and Elijah Fisher.
I love you all dearly!! Love, Nanna**

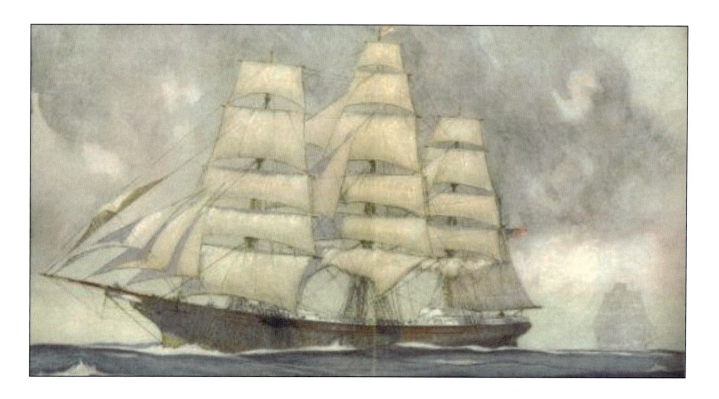

Printed in the United States of America.

Made in the USA
Middletown, DE
04 April 2023

28192384R00022